AF228552

FERRARI

A&D Xtreme
BOLD HI-LO NONFICTION
An imprint of Abdo Publishing
abdobooks.com

S.L. HAMILTON

ABDOBOOKS.COM

Published by Abdo Publishing, a division of ABDO, PO Box 398166, Minneapolis, Minnesota 55439. Copyright © 2023 by Abdo Consulting Group, Inc. International copyrights reserved in all countries. No part of this book may be reproduced in any form without written permission from the publisher. A&D Xtreme™ is a trademark and logo of Abdo Publishing.

Printed in the United States of America, North Mankato, MN.
052022
092022

Editor: John Hamilton

Copy Editor: Tamara L. Britton

Graphic Design: Sue Hamilton

Cover Design: Laura Graphenteen

Cover Photo: Shutterstock

Interior Photos & Illustrations: All photos Ferrari S.p.A., except:
Alamy-pgs 8-9 & 20-21; Getty/iStock-pgs 12-13, 14-15, 16-17, 22-23, 36-37 & 40-41; Shutterstock-pgs 4 (inset), 24-25, 26-27, 28-29 & 32-33; Wikimedia-pgs 7, 8 (inset), 27 (inset) & 39 (inset).

LIBRARY OF CONGRESS CONTROL NUMBER: 2021942644

PUBLISHER'S CATALOGING-IN-PUBLICATION DATA

Names: Hamilton, S.L., author.

Title: Ferrari / by S.L. Hamilton

Description: Minneapolis, Minnesota : Abdo Publishing, 2023 | Series: Xtreme cars | Includes online resources and index.

Identifiers: ISBN 9781532196065 (lib. bdg.) | ISBN 9781098216993 (ebook)

Subjects: LCSH: Ferrari automobile--Juvenile literature. | Sports cars--Juvenile literature. | Cars (Automobiles)--Juvenile literature.

Classification: DDC 629.2221--dc23

TABLE OF CONTENTS

CHAPTER 1

PRANCING HORSE CARS

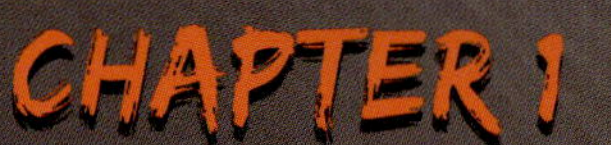

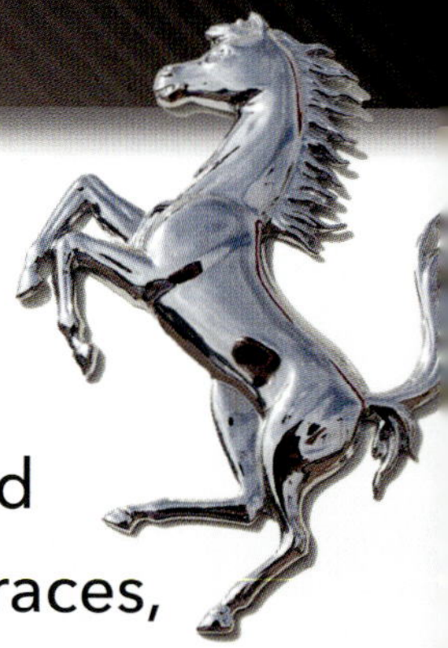

Ferraris are called "Prancing Horse" cars because of their well-known **logo**. Built in Italy, these **luxury** sports cars are beautiful and lightning fast. Ferraris have won hundreds of races, as well as the hearts of world-class and everyday drivers.

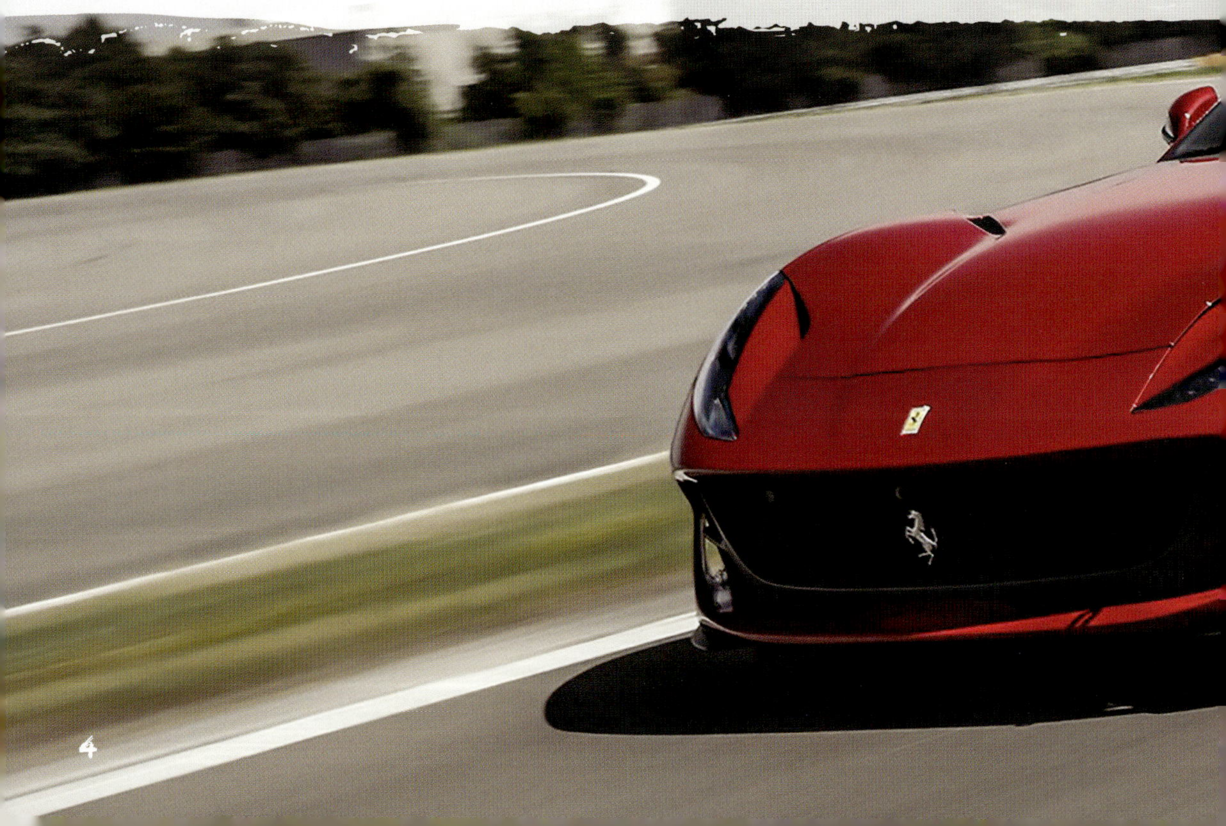

Ferrari 812 Superfast

CHAPTER 2

FERRARI'S HISTORY

Enzo Ferrari began racing in 1919, after World War I. By 1923, he won his first **Grand Prix** in Ravenna, Italy. However, Enzo stopped racing when two drivers he knew died in accidents. He formed Team Scuderia Ferrari (Ferrari stables) in 1929 in Modena, Italy. His job was to match drivers with Alfa Romeo cars.

By 1933, Enzo headed up Alfa Romeo's official racing department. But he wanted more. In 1939, Enzo left Alfa Romeo and started his own company.

Team Scuderia Ferrari was known by the Prancing Horse **logo**. The emblem was in honor of Italy's top World War I fighter pilot, Francesco Baracca. His family coat of arms had a prancing horse, which Baracca used on his planes. The flying ace died in action just before the end of the war. His family encouraged Enzo Ferrari to use the logo.

Francesco Baracca with the prancing horse emblem on his plane.

The Team Scuderia Ferrari's Prancing Horse logo was first seen on Alfa Romeo cars.

With the start of World War II, Ferrari's company began
making machine tools and aircraft parts for the war effort.
When Enzo's building was bombed twice, he moved the

company to Maranello, Italy, where it remains today. After the war's end in 1945, the Ferrari company returned to building race cars. The first was the 125 S in 1947.

CHAPTER 3

FERRARI RACE CARS

The first **Formula 1 (F1)** World Championship **Grand Prix** season took place in 1950. Scuderia Ferrari is the only team that has competed every season since the beginning. Driver Alberto Ascari won in 1952 and 1953, racing a Ferrari 375 and 500. In 2021, drivers Carlos Sainz and Charles Leclerc competed in a Ferrari SF21.

FERRARI FORMULA 1 SPECIFICATIONS

YEARS PRODUCED
1950-Present

MAXIMUM HORSEPOWER
1,000 (SF21 model)

ZERO TO 60 MPH (97 KPH)
2.6 seconds (SF21 model)

With new aerodynamic styling, the SF21 reaches speeds of 198.65 (319.7 kph).

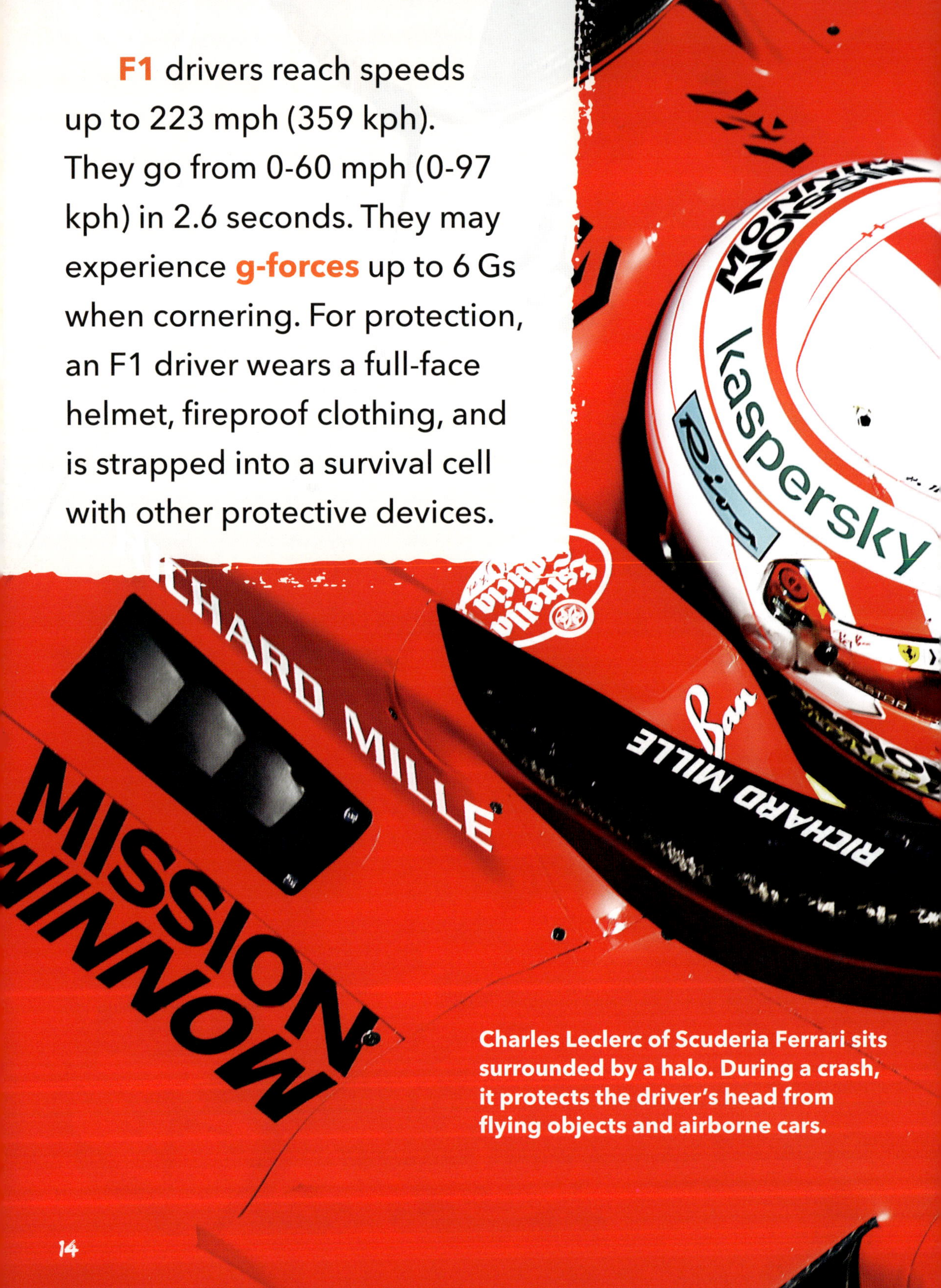

F1 drivers reach speeds up to 223 mph (359 kph). They go from 0-60 mph (0-97 kph) in 2.6 seconds. They may experience **g-forces** up to 6 Gs when cornering. For protection, an F1 driver wears a full-face helmet, fireproof clothing, and is strapped into a survival cell with other protective devices.

Charles Leclerc of Scuderia Ferrari sits surrounded by a halo. During a crash, it protects the driver's head from flying objects and airborne cars.

Halo

In Le Mans racing, 2- or 3-person teams drive sports cars on a track for up to 24 hours. Drivers switch out at pit stops. The winning team covers the greatest distance. The Ferrari 166 MM Barchetta became the winner of France's 24 Hours of Le Mans in 1949. Luigi Chinetti was at the wheel. In 2021, Ferrari teams continued **endurance racing** in a 488 GTE.

Drivers James Calado, Alessandro Pier Guidi, and Côme Ledogar raced #51 AF Corse Ferrari 488 GTE Evo during 2021's 24 Hours of Le Mans.

The Ferrari Challenge racing season finishes with the Finali Mondiali (World Finals) in Tuscany, Italy.

Ferrari Challenge races are competitions among drivers in specific models of Ferrari road cars. Races are held in Europe, North America, and Asia-Pacific regions.

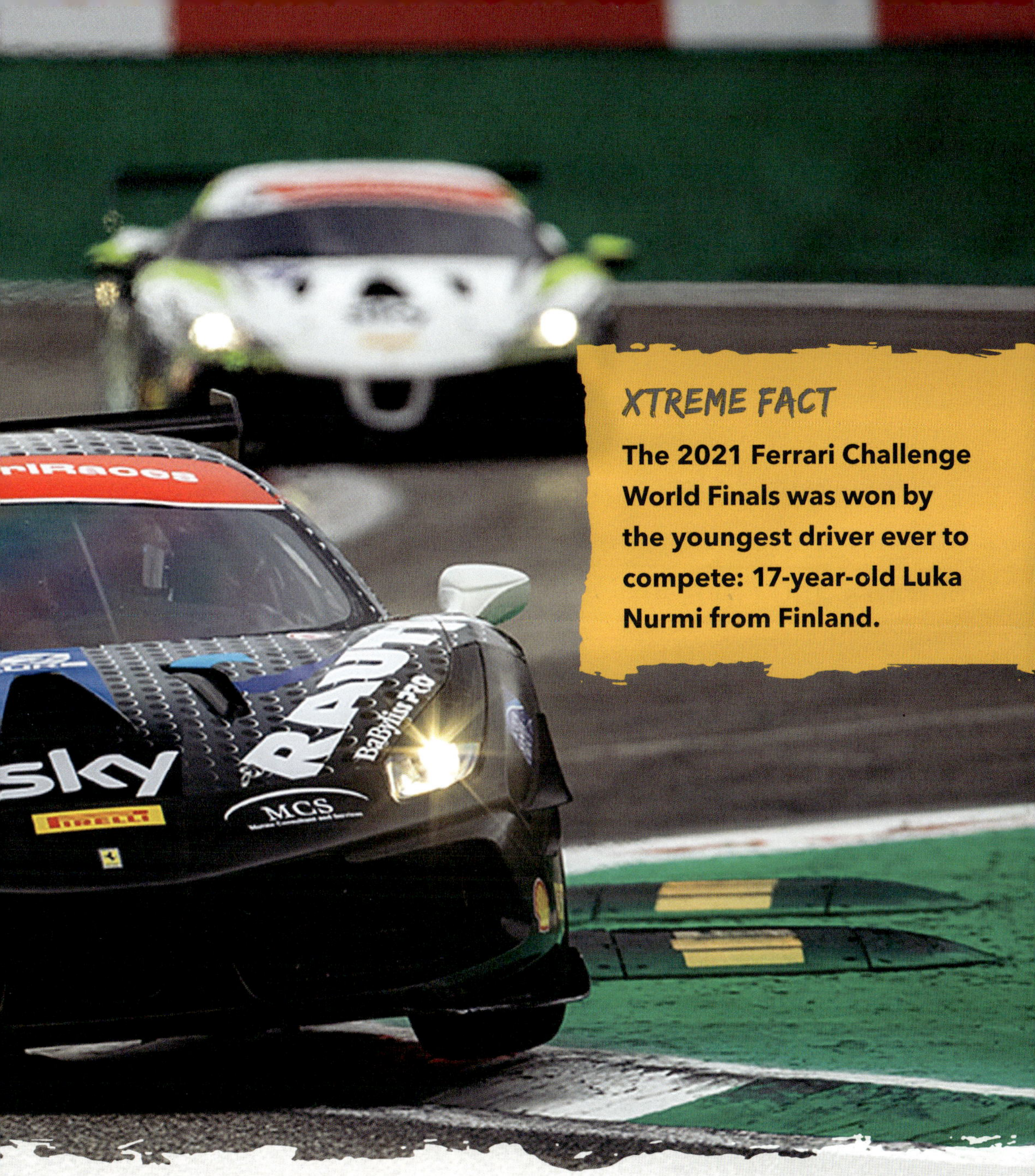

The first Ferrari-only race began in 1993 with Ferrari 348s.
New model Ferraris raced every few years. In 2021, drivers
competed against each other in Ferrari 488 Challenge Evos.

CHAPTER 4

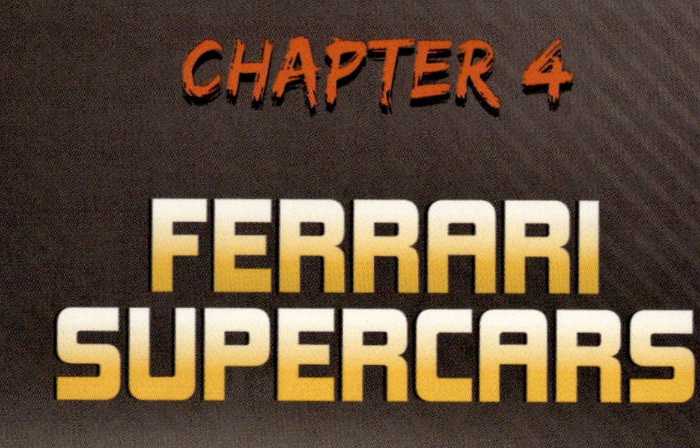

FERRARI SUPERCARS

A supercar offers world-class performance with speed, handling, and a unique design. Built from 1964-1966, Ferrari's 250 LM is an early supercar. The V12 engine had a race-winning top speed of 180 mph (290 kph).

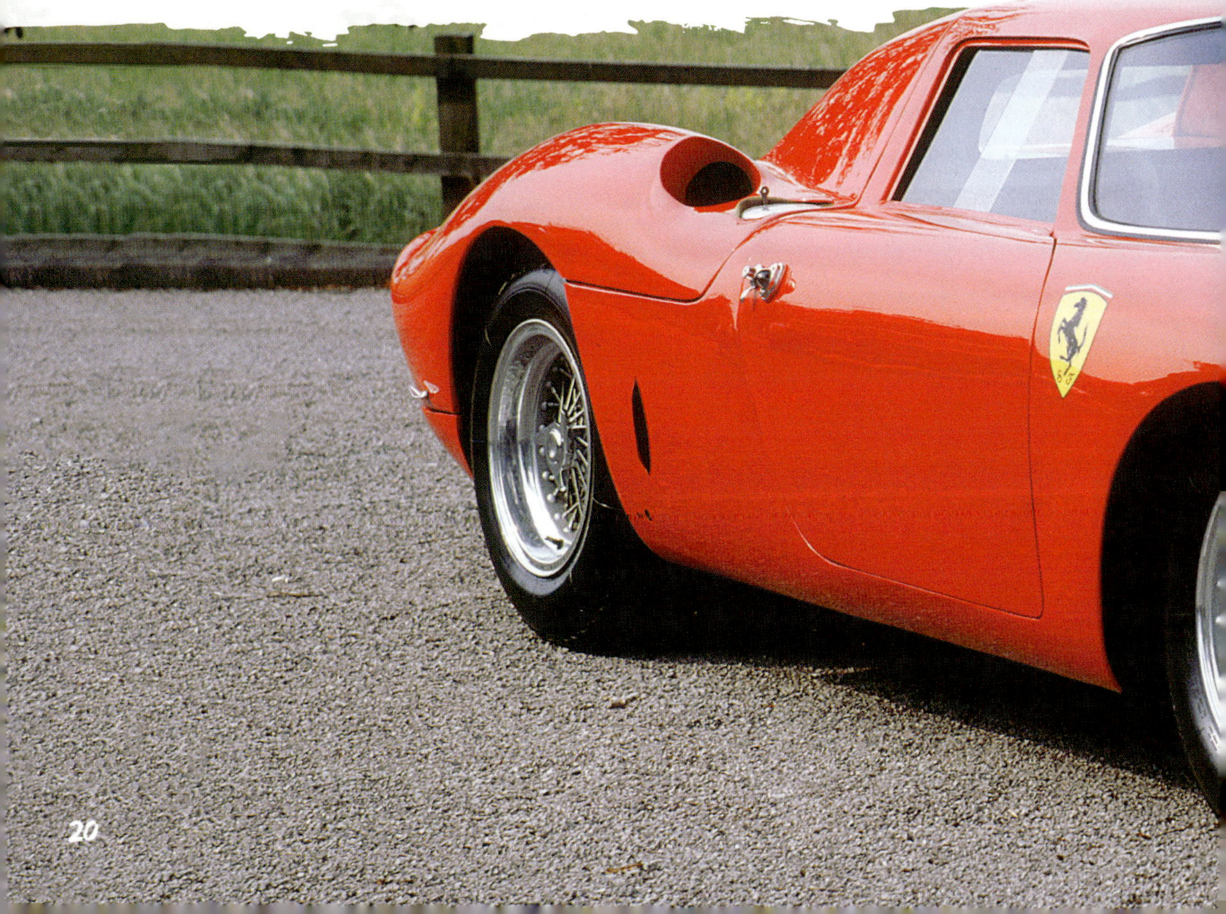

250 LM SPECIFICATIONS

YEARS PRODUCED
1964-1966

MAXIMUM HORSEPOWER
320 (1964 model)

ZERO TO 60 MPH (97 KPH)
4.5 seconds (1964 model)

The 250 LM was the last Ferrari to win the 24 Hours of Le Mans in 1965. The "LM" in the supercar's name stands for "Le Mans."

JM 265

The Berlinetta Boxer (BB) was made from 1973-1984. The wedge-shaped supercar featured a mid-mounted V12 engine placed behind the driver.

The 512 BB was both a race car and a road car. Ferrari built a total of 929 of these supercars.

Several Berlinetta Boxer models were made. The 512 BB supercar went from 0-60 mph (97 kph) in 4.9 seconds. It had a top speed of 188 mph (303 kph).

XTREME FACT

It took years for engineers to convince Enzo Ferrari to produce a mid-engine V12 supercar. He thought the car should follow the engine. But mid-engine cars were winning races, so he finally agreed to the change.

Testarossa was Ferrari's replacement for the 512 BB. The beautiful supercar was produced from 1984-1996. Its **aerodynamic** styling featured "cheese grater" **side strakes**. The V12 engine powered it from 0-60 mph (97 kph) in 5.2 seconds.

Testarossa is Italian for "red head." The supercar's most popular color was red, but it also came in white, black, silver, yellow, blue, and green.

The 550 Maranello's design put the V12 engine to the front of the car, where Enzo Ferrari preferred it. Built from 1996-2002, the 2-seater supercar had a top speed of 199 mph (320 kph). It went from 0-60 mph (97 kph) in 4.4 seconds.

The 550 Maranello had a leather interior and a traditional alloy gear shifter.

The F12 Berlinetta was awarded
Supercar of the Year in 2012 and
International Engine of the Year in
2013 by *Top Gear* magazine.

The F12 Berlinetta was introduced in 2012. It blasted from 0-60 mph (97 kph) in 3.1 seconds. Its top speed was 211 mph (340 kph). Drivers found the award-winning supercar both thrilling and easy to drive.

GRAND TOURERS

Grand tourers (GT) are cars that can be driven on public roads. Ferrari's America series were grand touring cars built from 1950-1967. The comfortable **coupes** and **roadsters** featured performance engines. Some were two-person cars and others were 2+2 (two people in the front and two in the back).

The 1951 Ferrari 340 America roadster had a top speed of 149 mph (240 kph).

AMERICA SPECIFICATIONS

YEARS PRODUCED
1950-1967

MAXIMUM HORSEPOWER
300 (1963 330 America model)

ZERO TO 60 MPH (97 KPH)
5.7 seconds (1963 330 model)

A 1963 330 America coupe grand tourer with 2+2 seating. It had a top speed of 160 mph (258 kph).

The Dino 206 and 246 GT were Ferrari's V6 grand tourers. Built from 1967-1974, the mid-engine road cars had a top speed of 146 mph (235 kph). The 206 GT was the first of Ferrari's cars built on an assembly line.

A 1969 Dino 246 GT had a longer body and a larger engine than the earlier 206 GT.

XTREME FACT

The name "Dino" was in honor
of Enzo Ferrari's son, who died
of muscular dystrophy while
designing the car's engine.

Ferrari's Mondial series was built from 1980-1993. These grand tourers featured a mid-engine V8. Cars came as either a 2+2 **coupe** or cabriolet (convertible). To increase power to the engine, Ferrari made a quattrovalvole. The engine had 4 valves per cylinder instead of 2. This created a grand tourer with 240 **horsepower (HP)** and a top speed of 149 mph (240 kph).

The 1983 Mondial cabriolet was Ferrari's first convertible in 9 years. Its folding canvas roof was cleverly hidden behind the rear seats.

The Mondial's hood-wide, air-louvered front vents and stylish side intake vents helped cool its V8 engine.

The Ferrari F40 was made from 1987-1992. The sporty grand tourer celebrated the Ferrari company's 40th anniversary. Its strong but lightweight body was built of

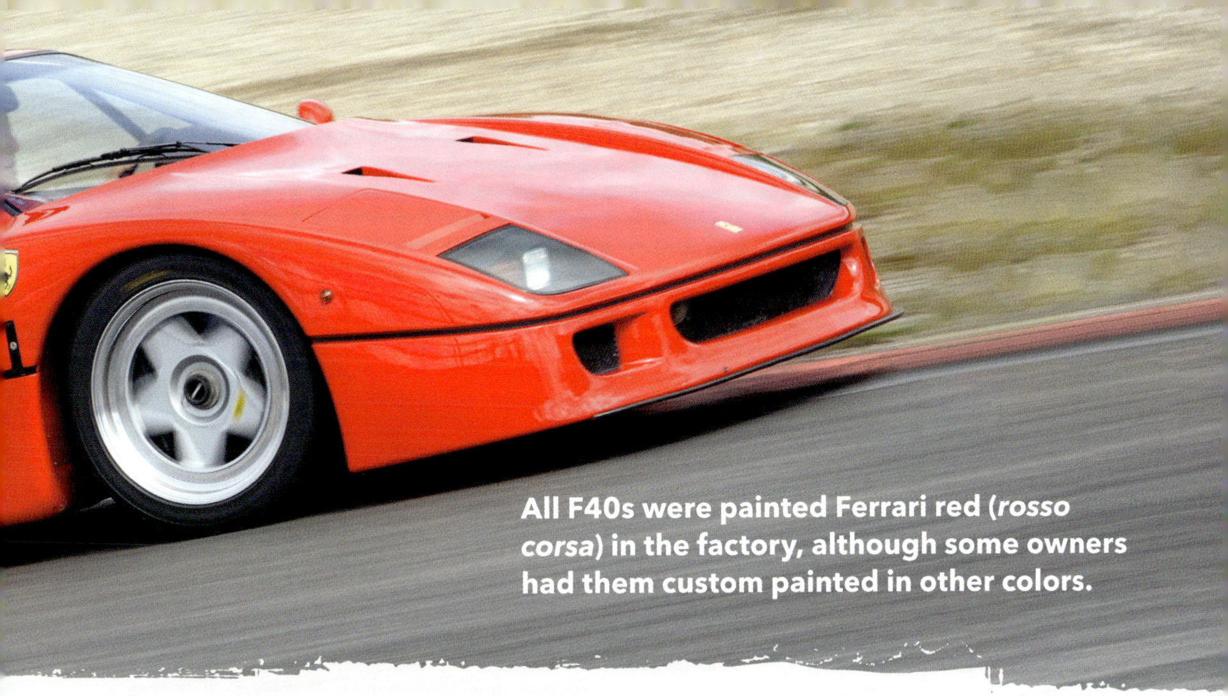

All F40s were painted Ferrari red (*rosso corsa*) in the factory, although some owners had them custom painted in other colors.

Kevlar, carbon fiber, and aluminum. With a mid-engine V8 and 471 **HP**, the F40 had a fiery top speed of 201 mph (324 kph). It was the fastest and most powerful Ferrari to date.

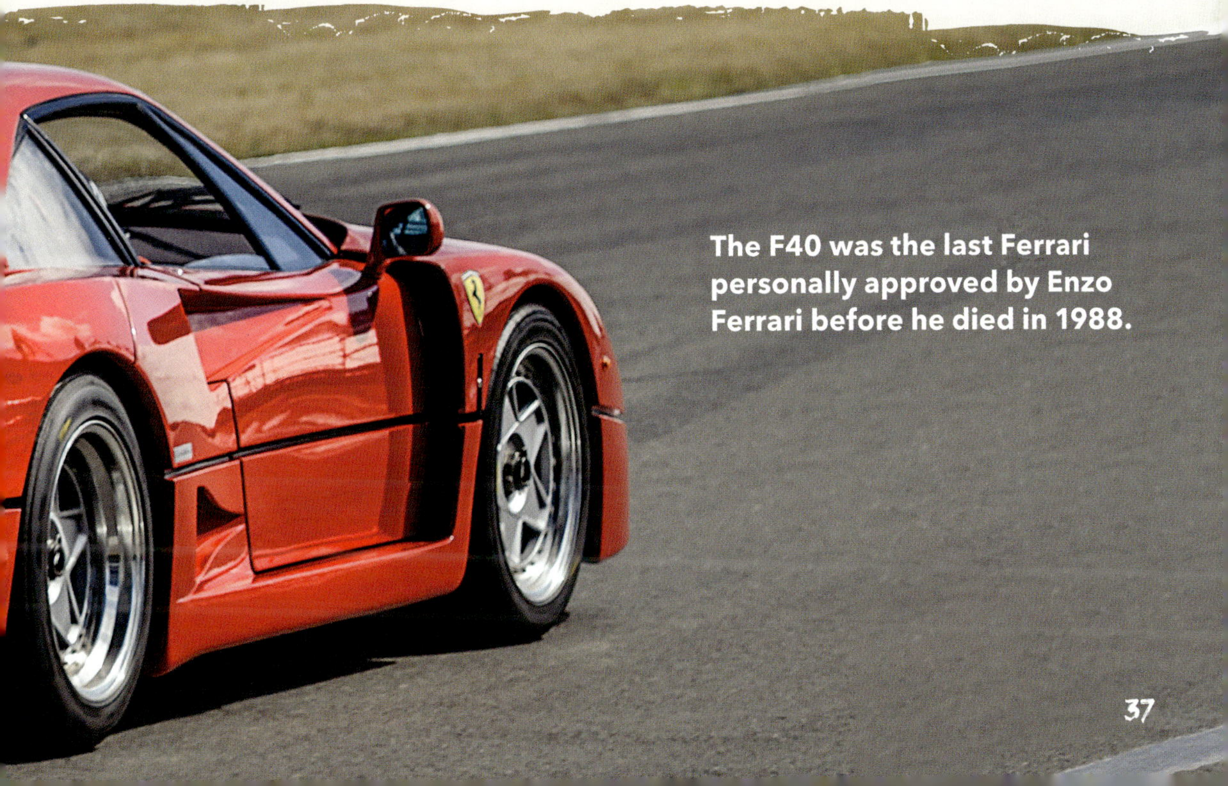

The F40 was the last Ferrari personally approved by Enzo Ferrari before he died in 1988.

The F430 Scuderia was built from 2004-2009. It mixed the lightweight, powerful traits of a race car with a grand tourer. With clean, **aerodynamic** lines and a lighter weight, the F430 was designed for maximum performance.

The F430 Scuderia's V8 engine brought the grand tourer's top speed to 198 mph (319 kph).

For the first time in 2004, the F430 had a **manettino switch** on the steering wheel. This allowed the driver better control of the vehicle.

Manettino
Switch

XTREME FACT

Seven-time world champion race car driver Michael Schumacher was involved in the engineering and testing of the F430 Scuderia.

CHAPTER 6

FERRARI HYPERCARS

Hypercars take acceleration and speed beyond all others. Ferrari created this with LaFerrari, meaning "The Ferrari," or the ultimate Ferrari. As Ferrari's first hybrid **production car**, the electric motor combined with the V12 engine to reach a blazing top speed of 217 mph (350 kph).

With its hybrid engine, LaFerrari is said to have "Two Beating Hearts."

LAFERRARI
SPECIFICATIONS

YEARS PRODUCED
2013-2018

MAXIMUM HORSEPOWER
949 (LaFerrari model)

ZERO TO 60 MPH (97 KPH)
2.4 seconds (LaFerrari model)

The LaFerrari Aperta is an open-top model built from 2016-2018 to celebrate the 70th anniversary of the Ferrari company. The hypercar features redirected airflow around the body to create the same 217 mph (350 kph) lightning-fast speed as the hardtop LaFerrari.

Aperta is Italian for "open." Although an open top, a LaFerrari Aperta comes with both a carbon-fiber hardtop and a canvas soft top.

XTREME FACT

Certain Ferrari customers were invited to buy a LaFerrari Aperta. All models were presold by the time it was introduced at the 2016 Paris Motor Show in France.

CHAPTER 7

THE FUTURE

Ferrari's future is plug-in hybrid electric vehicles such as the SF90 Stradale. The environmentally friendly hypercar has a top speed of 211 mph (340 kph). With **aerodynamic** designs and super speed, Ferrari merges power and beauty into greener race and **production cars**.

An SF90 Stradale. The name is Italian for "made for the road."

XTREME CHALLENGE

1) What is the nickname for Ferrari cars?

2) Who started the Ferrari company? In what country?

3) Ferrari's racing team is known as Scuderia Ferrari. What does that mean in English?

4) What was the first Ferrari car? What year was it built?

5) In what two back-to-back years did Scuderia Ferrari driver Alberto Ascari win the Formula 1 World Championship Grand Prix?

6) Which Ferrari supercar had "cheese grater" side strakes? What years was it built?

7) Some Ferrari Grand Tourers have 2+2 seating. What does that mean?

8) What is a hypercar? Name a Ferrari model hypercar.

GLOSSARY

aerodynamic – Something that has a shape that reduces the drag, or resistance, of air moving across its surface. Cars with aerodynamic shapes can go faster because they don't have to push as hard to get through the air.

coupe – A passenger car with a fixed roof that cannot be removed, usually with two or three doors. Coupes have a sportier look than four-door sedans, with a sloping rear roofline.

endurance racing – An auto race that requires drivers and their cars to handle many hours of near-constant driving.

Formula One (F1) – A single-seat, super-fast racing vehicle. F1 cars are typically raced on racetracks or road courses.

g-force – A unit of force placed on a body when it is subjected to acceleration. The force is felt as increasing weight. The pull of Earth's gravity equals one g-force.

Grand Prix – An auto race where drivers are in a single-seat racing car with uncovered wheels.

horsepower (HP) – A unit of measure of power. The term was originally invented to compare the power output by a steam engine with that of an average draft horse.

Kevlar – A light and very strong man-made fiber.

logo – A graphic symbol that identifies a company.

luxury – Something that adds pleasure or comfort, and is often expensive.

manettino switch – A dial on a Ferrari steering wheel that can be switched by the driver to adjust the electronics of a car's suspension. *Manettino* is Italian for "little lever."

production car – A model of car that is produced by a company that all look the same and are sold to the public.

roadster – A car with an open roof that seats two people.

side strakes – A design feature on the side of a car door that helps direct airflow, aiding in aerodynamics and cooling the engine.

ONLINE RESOURCES

To learn more about Ferraris, please visit **abdobooklinks.com** or scan this QR code. These links are routinely monitored and updated to provide the most current information available.

INDEX